Inspiration
with a Chuckle

Simon Sez:
Look for it here

Told by Simon Stargazer III

By James W. Haworth

authorHOUSE®

AuthorHouse™
1663 Liberty Drive
Bloomington, IN 47403
www.authorhouse.com
Phone: 1 (800) 839-8640

Published by AuthorHouse   02/11/2017

ISBN: 978-1-5246-5468-9 (sc)
ISBN: 978-1-5246-5467-2 (e)

Library of Congress Control Number: 2016920586

Print information available on the last page.

Credits

Cover: Star Field Photo
Astronomy-NASA-hubble-space-picture-heaven-merope2

Cover: Earth Photo
Courtesy, NASA

Cover Design:
James W. Haworth and Glen T. Lindahl

Photographic Illustrations:
James W. Haworth

Photo of Author:
Patricia E. Altman (Author's wife)

Inspiration for pen name, Simon Stargazer III:
Luke Skywalker from the movie Star Wars

First line of critique:
Patricia E. Altman

Foreword
(I didn't know I was a writer.)
How do you come up with "Inspiration with a chuckle"?

English was always one of my least favorite subjects. Even in High School Sophomore English, when in a flash of effervescent brilliance, I earned an A+ on a descriptive assignment, I remained singularly unimpressed with the whole thing; (Circa 1956)

Fast forward to 1984, please. In a stroke of temporary brilliance, I purchased a Macintosh computer because I was too lazy to learn PC programing and computing at the time. The ease of use, provided by the Mac, opened the worlds of my imagination. Over the next twenty years, I played around and dabbled with very short, but descriptive thoughts that leave a distinct impression. (also, known as aphorisms) I also wrote short story lines that frequently had a surprise ending.

A new job in 2001 allowed me to test out my aphorisms on a new and unexpecting audience. Not wanting to identify myself just yet, I put a new saying, signed by Simon Stargazer III, on each of about ten work stations before the work day started.

I did this several times a week for about two years before someone finally figured out who the author was. It wasn't long before a colleague suggested that I start a blog to expand my reach. I did. It also didn't take long for someone to suggest that I write a book of positive thoughts with a humorous bent.

Oh, boy! I sure didn't think that I wanted to work that hard! Long story, short, it took me two years, but in 2006, I finally got my first book of sayings published. A few sold, but I wound up giving away most of the copies of "Wit and Wisdom from the Wild and Wacky World of Simon Stargazer III"

In the intervening years, I went on to publish three more works, each of which not only contained sayings, but poems and short stories as well. These were to be eclectic collections that hopefully would appeal to a wider range of readers. (I still wound up giving away most of my books.) My advice: don't give up your day job, and especially, don't expect to retire on your book royalties.

Now, ten years later, I return to the original format of just including short wise or witty sayings that leave an impact. I have culled some of the best sayings from the first four books, as well as new sayings written during the past four years.

It is my hope that this little book will both amuse and inspire my readers to look for the best in life and each other. If I have made one person smile, try something new, or just persevere, then my job will have been worth the effort.

Jim Haworth
AKA Simon Stargazer III

Dedication

This book is dedicated to the memory of my friend, mentor and computer guru, Gary Terrell.

Contents

Chapter One
Starting at the Beginning

Chapter Two
Decision Making

Chapter Three
Love is a Many Splendored Thing

Chapter Four
Nuggets of Truth to Consider

Chapter Five
Other Points to Ponder

Chapter Six
Be Smart... Or Else!

Chapter Seven
Dichotomy & Other Persasions

Chapter Eight
Acronyms to live by
(Taken from Simon Sez: You're the Expert on You)

Chapter Nine
Impatience

Chapter Ten
Patience

Chapter Eleven
Time

Chapter Twelve
Getting Old

Chapter Thirteen
Where do we go from here

Chapter Fourteen
I Can't Get It Out of My Head!

Chapter Fifteen
Warnings

Chapter Sixteen
What should I do about The Past?

Chapter Seventeen
At Last!

Chapter Eighteen
Consider God

Chapter One
Starting at the Beginning

Work

Honest work,
At no matter, what level,
Can be an inspiring teaching tool

It's a Good Start, Charlie

It's a good start, Charlie Brown...
Attitude drives actitude!

(yes, I made that word up, but it works)

The Journey of a Lifetime

The
Journey
Of a lifetime
Begins with knowledge...
So, you need to stock up on it early!

Reality

Reality is perception that is unfiltered.

Reactions

Reactions are driven by actions!
Serious consideration should be given
Before you let your self be driven.

Look-alike

You may have a look-alike, but
Your values are yours alone.

Plans

If
The
Best
Laid plans
Of Mice and Men
Are mostly incompatible.
They need to pick better partners!

Life **is**
About choices;
<u>Spend more time</u>
On the really big ones!

LIFE IS A FORCE to be reckoned with...
So, you better just get with it!

Live Life one day at a time;
it works better that way.

When you get weary
Remember... It's only 24 hours,
And then you get a fresh start all over again

Never Forget:

Pound for Pound,
There's nothing like enthusiasm!

If you want to win it:
You must get involved in it!

Everyone gets their buttons pushed
How we react defines us as a person.

Heated passion
is rarely about fashion!

Claiming to be
More than you are
Won't get you far!

Speaking your mind

Is a lot like cutting boards:
Measure twice before
Opening mouth

My advice: Say it nice!

Being a
One-man team
Rarely works well

You cannot
Lead without presence

Life is worth more living
When it's all about giving

The longer you live
The shorter it gets, but
<u>The richer it becomes</u>

And remember this:

Don't fold
Just 'cause
You're old!

As the years go by
You can be quite sure
His love will endure

Look at life
With the reverence
Of laughter

Life is already too short
Don't make it any shorter

Time is a lot like change
But it just never stops

Life is a good learning experience
For what comes next.

If
You
Can do
Better, then
Why aren't you??

Think about that for a while!

Though our Blessings
Are too numerous
To count
We can
Still
Try

Attitude
Can be your
Fountain of youth... *Think about it!*

Everyone
Has a benchmark
They want to live up to.
Did you set yours high enough?
From time to time I wonder about mine!

Persistence

If you want something bad enough,
Be as persistent as the wind.
It always comes back.

The
Distance
Between two
Points does not
Really matter if you are
Fully determined to get there.

Live for now, but
Plan for a "future now"
(Inspired by a Pepsi ad, of all things!)

Be passionate
It's more fun
Than being angry

One
Of the
Most positive
Thoughts you can
Have is in your smile!

We do not choose to be born. We do, however,
Make the choices that set the course of our life!

Inspired by a line from the film "Lincoln"

Education

An education is essential...
What you do with it can be priceless.
Especially if you use essential discernment!

Watch Out for Wisdom

Wisdom
May result from the
Conscientious application of

Focused perception

Morning

If
the
best
time of
your day
is morning
Go to bed early!

Enthusiasm and Excellence

Enthusiasm
Coupled with excellence is

Rarely stoppable

The Journey II

The journey
of a thousand miles
may start with the first step,
But the real journey of a lifetime
Begins with inspired determination!

Sometimes Getting There is...

Sometimes
Getting there is more
Fun than actually being there

Life Changes

Change with it till you fit
Or change it till it fits you!

My Dad always said

"If you're going to do something, do it right"
I might add "But you have to get up and go do it!"

Fun

If you're
Not having fun
You need to start over!

Learn

Learn more
To live longer!

If you can

If ya can think it...
I bet ya can do it!

Importance!

You
Define
Your own
Importance!

Celebrate

Celebrate every day
Like it's your birthday,
For it's God's Gift to you
Each day. Happy Gift Day!

Green

Green will grow on you,
Especially if you're standing still.
So, you might think about getting moving!

Procrastination

When
I want to
Procrastinate
I play a learning game*
That way, at least it's not a
Total waste of my precious time!

>*Like Words with Friends
>(On the internet)

The Future

Don't
Let the lack of
A past... frame your future.

(important when considering a new venture)

Today

Thank you, Lord,
For this day You've given me.

I'll try to do at least one
Positive thing with it.

If

If
you
think
you can...
Just go for it!
You might surprise some
and confirm the expectations of others!

Who Are You?

You
Are the
Sum of your
Experience. Use it
To the best of your ability!!

Inspired by a scene from
"Signed, Sealed and Delivered"
A series on the Hallmark Channel on Cable TV

The Door to Your Future

The door to adventure
Is always open, and it
Starts with education

The door to adventure:

Olney Friends School, Barnesville, Ohio

Chapter Two
Decision Making

Life
Takes
Courage
To live right

Life on the edge
Is the essence of discovery!

Discovery often happens
In unfamiliary territory!

Discernment is knowing
When to step into that
Unfamiliar territory!

Courage is what it takes
To act on that discernment
(sometimes under fire)

Determination is what
Drives you to accomplish the goal

What you do with your brain
Determines what your mind becomes

Practice, and change
Keeps the mind sharp

You know you're alive and functional
If your body can carry your mind around

Neither government's watchful eyes and ears nor their powers of seduction, are any match for the computerized facial recognition surveilance programs being designed for and in use by big business to attract and messmerize customers.

Regardless of all this expense and effort, it is still up to the consumers to decide whether or not to buy what either party is trying to sell us.

We

Make

Choices

Regardless

Of others voices

And the results are

Our own responsibilities.

Learn from all you encounter;
Use that knowledge with care and respect

Learn when to
Cut your ties

> Life is too short
> To be tied to people
> Who fear you for your past

> Life is too short
> To be tied to people
> Who wish to ignore you

> Life is too short
> To be tied to people
> Who don't want you around

> Life is too short
> To be tied to people
> Who only want to use you

> Life is too short
> Not to learn to just be you
> The ones who see will love you

> Let your inside light
> Shine outside

In short, life is too short not to learn from it.

Perception is altered reality

Perception changes
Reality doesn't
Success in life
Relies upon careful
Scrutiny of reality with
A healthy re-evaluation of...
You guessed it: *your perception.*

Sometimes

Life
Takes
A turn

Will you
Be ready???

Need Help with Trouble?

If you think
You've got trouble...
Think again... and again.
The third time's the charm!
You can think your way out of it!

Buttons Pushed?

Everyone gets their buttons pushed...
How we react to it defines us.

Responsibility...

Be responsible for your actions
For surely there'll be reactions!

Green

The green in my yard
Has me out numbered (And... I love it!)

*Besides... the red, yellow, orange, white
and purple flowers that are also there!*

*How can you have thoughts of gloom?
When all the flowers are in bloom?*

Participation

Even
When you
Don't participate
You sometimes find that
You participated in a big way!

Next time, remember to vote!!

Utterances

A saying in the mouth
Is worth two in the brain

If you ponder the consequences
Before you boldly utter it!

That Look

If the look on your face
Says more than
Your lips...

Please be fully aware
Of the message!

Who Did You Say You Are?

You are the sum of
Your unique experience.
And as such can come up with
Completely different solutions than
Anyone else with similar experience!

Procrastination Revisited

The best procrastination is when
I come up with a really great idea
While avoiding what I must do!

(How about you?)

Preservatives or not?

If preservatives are used to
preserve the food we eat...

Why won't they preserve us?
Simple... we're not dead yet!

But...

They might make us that way
somewhat prematurely, dont'cha think?

Buy organic when you can
Fresh food is a good plan.

Here's my advice;
Check label twice!

Frugality

Before you shop...
Prepare a prop.

I really must insist
You make a good list

Give some thought
Before it's bought.

For, if by impulse you're lead
It might just put you in the red!

Choices

Every thing
You do in life
Involves a choice.

Informed
Choices
Can lead to
A better life

Chapter Three
Love is a Many Splendored Thing

True
Love is
An irrevocably
Insatiable commitment.
And it is rewarding as well!

Love is
A heart attack
That <u>some</u> people
Just never get over!

Love is like a cool shady pond
In the middle of a hidden glen

A nifty place for you and your
Sweetheart to quietly dip in

My valentine warms my heart
Even in the winter's icy start
(written for my wife Pat in

The heart of Winter)

In my heart, I love you.

Elixirs:

Water may be
The elixir of life but...
Love is the elixir of humanity!

Love Transends Technology

The written page may crumble
Your computer may crash and
Your cell phone battery may die...

But, face to face, you'll still be able
To tell your sweetheart how much
You love her, as the days go by.

Young Love:

Love's early phase
With it's adoring gaze

The Fourteenth

I say!
The 14th should be...
Valentines day every month.
We need a lot more love in the world!

One
Good
Turn can
Change a life

Miracles
Happen every day
The trick is to be a there.
Or even better: be a part of them!

Smiles are the universal language...
Use them liberally in every encounter.

Your smile is a gift from God
That you deliver personally.

The smile is an
External expression
Of your internal intention

You can
Send a smile
To someone by phone
And brighten the rest of their day!

Inspired by the Family Circus cartoon by Bill and Jeff Keane
Printed in the Indianapolis Star on 11/22/2013

Let your smile radiate!

**True love
Can be a pain
In the butt, and yet
It's totally worth it all!**

Chapter Four
Nuggets of Truth to Consider

Longing is
An integral
Part of living

Aspiration is
Longing focused.

Education is
The vehicle of
Achievement

The goodness you do will live on
Through the lives of those you affect

In this manner the efforts of your mind
Will transcend the limits of time itself.

That Spark

Everyone
Has that Spark
Of goodness within...

You may be the one
Called upon to nurture it.

The Human Brain

The human brain is like a black hole,
Constantly pulling information in that
It never forgets... the problem is that you
May later forget where it is stored.

The act
Of writing
Your thoughts
Tends to clarify them

Everyone has Pros and Cons

Progress is made when you
Emphasize the pros
And modify the cons.

Life is Love

Life is love, a works in progress...
Accompanied by dirt, smells and experience.
Change what you need to and can, then enjoy the rest!

Watch out for Wisdom... Extended

Wisdom
May result from the
Conscientious application of
Focused perception, which
Can be applied anywhere
(and any time)

Along Came a Spider...

Spiders are God's adrenalin booster!

Don't Try it!

Don't try to
Get on your horse
Before the saddle's in place
Unless you're a good bare back rider!

Think about how that might apply to your life.

Bad Days

Bad days may be more
Opportune than good ones...
They allow you to think of solutions
You might never have even considered.

Crying rinses out the soul.

Every Day is

Every day is
A beautiful day
Attitude makes it so

What is a Waste of Energy?

You
Know:
<u>Anger</u> is a
Stupendous
Waste of energy
Especially since the
Person it is directed at
May not even be aware of it!

The Best Substitute for Experience

The best substitute for Experience
Is the ability to follow instructions!

When Grief Comes

When grief comes
Into your heart embrace it
For it will make more room for love

A small goal every day
Can build your life
In every way!

When Building Accomplishments

When
Building
Accomplishments
Start small to leave

Room for growth

That Accomplishment

That accomplishment
No matter how small
Builds confidence, and...

Greater confidence
Prepares you to tackle
Bigger accomplishments

Great Truths... are simple concepts.

The Rainbow is

Nature's reminder that
Beauty can be raindrop deep.

Blue Skies

Blue skies
Remind us why we
Don't have to feel so blue.

Smiles

Smiles
Are truly the
Universal language

Success

Measure
Success by
How well you
Handle failures

Learn from the Past

We
need to
update our
door to the past,
to look for the beauty,
wisdom and strength that
we can find in our past memories,
associations and learning experiences.

Blue Skies re-visited

I worked 43 years in the dark,
Doing Echocardiography
Now I write and look
Out the window
At the sky.
I love it when
It's blue, but when
Its cloudy I imagine the
Blue above the clouds and smile!

Creativity

You cannot
Tie down the wild spirit...
Its creativity will inevitably out!
Find a way to encourage its positive flow.
Then just stand back and watch it's
blossoming!

Chores

Most chores
Are just bores

They don't have to be that way
They can be exciting every day!

Now take heed
Of what you'll need

Let your imagination soar
As you paint that old door

Pretend, pretend, and pretend!
It'll get you quickly to the end!

While vacuuming that expansive floor
You're a dirt-eating dragon looking for more!

And while you're mowing that lawn,
You're preparing for a duel at dawn!

You want it ever so smooth
When they make their move

Wouldn't want them to trip
When they finally let'er rip!

Well, now that you get the idea,
It's time for me to go... See ya!

People Are Beautiful

People are...
Beautiful in content
As well as appearance.
You should look inside sometime!

Handling A Little Stress...

A little stress comes into each life,
Not always caused by external strife

Some carry, locked in their mind,
Worries that others just never find

If it's something that can't be changed,
Please... don't let it make you deranged.

If it's someone else's problem,
Don't fret... just give it to 'em!

If they need help, well then, you can offer,
So long as it doesn't end up in your coffer.

But, if the problem is really yours,
Get in the boat and dig in your oars!

Make a plan and gather your resources.
See if YOU need help from other sources!

Solutions are reached by planned action,
While worry only produces distraction!

If You're Feelin' Blue

If you're feelin' blue
Here's what you do:

Take a trek through the
Corridors of your mind

To see what treasures
you can find

After a while
You'll find a smile

Grab it and give it away
You'll get it back all day!

Time Spent With a Purring Cat

Time spent with
A purring cat
Is life at
Its best
Rivaling
The adoring
Licks of a puppy

09/29/2006

Chapter Five
Other Points to Ponder

Perceptions

It may be that
What you perceive
Is what you believe

And it may be that
A change in perceptions
Results in a change to your life

Eyes

Eyes
Wide open
Admit more light
Brains work like that too

*Think about
the implications!*

When Taking a Walk, Remember

One small step for a man
May be just about right for a woman
(Or it could get your block knocked off!)

Old Ben Franklin said:

"A bird in the hand is worth two in the bush."

I
Say
A bird
In the hand
Was too darn slow!

Luck

Luck, good or bad
Is there to be had...

So look ahead and be prepared:
From luck you may be spared!

Fit or not...

Even tough blokes
Might have strokes

Lifetime

The longer you live
The shorter it gets!

Life's a Hoot!

Life's a Hoot...
Till ya get the boot!

So...

Use every hour you can...
Before they put you in one!

To Take Advantage of

Take advantage of Serendipity
Be as prepared as you can be!

Be Happy Like me

I'm
Happy
As a clam
No matter
Where I am!

(You think I should be institutionalized?)

A Sure Way

Sure way to miss old age
Is to practice road rage!

Twenty Four Hours

Twenty four hours is just barely
Enough time to get to tomorrow

Life's Way

It's what you do
Along the way

That matters most
Each and every day

Celebrate Life

Celebrate life like there's no tommorow
For, sooner or later, there will be no later!

TODAY is the day
That couldn't wait till tomorrow

TOMORROW is the day
That was too late for today

When You Need More

Do you need more than a tool?
It's time to go back to school!

Truman: A man of few words

A
sign
on his desk
said it quite clear:
The buck stops here!

Nothing New

Someone once said:
"There's nothing new under the sun."

I submit to you that:
There's a whole lotta new
Made from what was already here
And new ideas pop up every second
As new brains tackle old and new concepts.
From their fresh points of view with new tools

You Have to...

You have to get through today
Before you can be serious about tomorrow.

Always do more than is anticipated.
The reward may be more than you expected.

Pineapple Upside Down Cake

Do
You
Suppose?
Was pineapple
Upside down cake
Invented by accident?

Alhough our days are numbered,
We are assured that they will
Last till we are done with them.

Fog... is God's reminder to
slow down and arrive alive

Real
Beauty is
Heart deep

The Eye of the Camera

The Camera's eye reveals
The Mind of the
Photographer

Interestingly,
It reveals different things
To different people.

Truths Are
Great
Truths are
Uncomplicated

If You Can't...

If
You
Can't win
At least have
A good time trying!

Rainbows are
The color of life.

Life's
What you make it
Don't half bake it!

Wisdom

Words of
Wisdom are
Easy to come by
Learning to live by
Them is the hard part

Truth and Belief

Truth and belief
Are not the same.

Discernment helps
Transfer the former to...
The later

Scurriers

Humans are Scurriers...

They scurry here
They scurry there...

Pretty soon
They're everywhere!

Hopefully they'll learn to be more nice
Before they make it out beyond our skies.

Good
Friends
Never die
They just enrich
Your memories!

Wonderful!

Isn't it wonderful when
someone scratches an itch
you didn't even know you had?

Pondered Utterances

A saying in the mouth
Is worth two in the brain...

If you ponder the consequences
Before you boldly utter it.

Un-Communication

Communication is a two way street
Unfortunately, not usually very fleet!

Messages not passed,
Result in being last!

Demands made can be unfair
But sometimes I just don't care!

Temperatures may rise;
There's **FIRE** in the eyes!

Even someone who's a powderpuff
Starts to scream and leave in a huff!

People need to listen to others
Instead of ignoring who it bothers.

What you say under pressure
Is rarely meant to reassure

Slow down and be calm...
Understanding is a balm

Try not to get under their skin
You might have to work with them again!

Filled Brains

Our brains
Are all the same.
It's what we fill'em with
That makes such a difference.

Shared Knowledge

Knowledge shared
Can grow everyone it touches,
But that touch must be
Acknowledged to
Effect change.

Mother Nature

See
What
Mother
Nature can
Do without a brain...
Think what
All you'll
Do with
One!

**Sheep Sorrel
Growing out of a cleft
In a very large Maple tree**

Contageous Things

Smiles

Yawns

Colds

Goodness

Compliments

Enthusiasm

Confidence

Savor them...
And share the good ones!

Chapter Six
Be Smart... Or Else!

Be Smart

Don't be consumed by
Something you can't control!
If you can't go over it, under it, around it
Or change it, go to the guy who can, but have an
Impelling argument worthy of his time and consideration.

If...

If
It is
Worth it
Don't give up
On an uphill battle!

If not...

If not
Then find
Something else
To be excited about!

(See "Life is there", page after next)

Regardless of What...

Regardless of what
The government may say
You are the master of your destiny.

Progress

Progress
Is sometimes
The product of the

Patiently persistent push

Frozen Joy

The
Joy of
A heavy
Snowfall is
The almost total
Absence of NOISE (!!)
From the world around you!
Wait for it and enjoy it when it comes.
For the intrusive world of noise will be back.
(With a vengeance)

Life is there...

Life is there to be lived,
Whether you like it or not...
So, live like you love it to the end!

Consider this:

Many of us can count the number of
TRUE friends we have on the fingers of one hand

If having a problem with such a friend, think on this:
Would we rather lop off a finger or lop off a friend?

The inspired answer would be: Why would I do either...
I need all my friends and my fingers!

This doesn't just apply to "Five Finger Friends",
Now, does it?

Are you someone's FFF?

Understanding

Understanding
Comes with
Exposure
& Time

Frustration

In the interest of expediency,
Frustration must be controlled

ZIG-ZAG

Time is a straight line, but...

Life zigs

Then it zags.

Joy comes in meshing the two.

Simon Stargazer (Mar. '14 in NinePatch) says, "Editor Frances once said to me, 'There is a bright side to everything.' That is how I find my life's joy-in meshing the two.

I look for the beauty in each day the Lord has given me. It is always there to be found. (Some days the challenge is a lot harder than others.) The photo says it all: The Tree of Life may zig and it may zag, but it still reaches the sky-

And its great fun to climb!"

**A tree in front of Bundy Hall
On the campus of Earlham College,
Richmond, Indiana**

Success

Dwelling
On your successes
May be prideful, however...

Dwelling on your failures can be
Your motivation for new successes!

Brain Power

Sometimes
It takes more than
One brain to help another
Brain get the critical answers.

My son is almost done rehabbing his house. A friend and I have been helping. Many times, he has been puzzled to find a solution for a particular fix. The two of 'em would hash over the problem, and one of us would finally make an observation triggering a new line of thought.

<u>Three brains finally found a way.</u>

Flushing

Flushing as soon as
The poop hits the porcelain
Makes toilet cleaning easier later...

<u>*This works with life too!*</u>

Life Happens!

Life happens.
And if you don't happen with it
You may miss some great stuff!!

Limits

Know your limits...
Otherwise how can you
Expect to exceed them?

Persistence Knows

Persistence
Knows no limits
And it usually pays well

Anger

Anger
Nibbles
At your soul.
Don't let it eat too much.

Comfort Zone

The only
Way to expand
Your comfort zone is
To go outside it more often

Enthusiasm

Uncurbed enthusiasm is better than
Uncurbed pessimism any day of the week!

Advice

**My
Advice:
Say it nice!**

(That's important enough to read all by itself)

Power

Will power
Works better than
Won't power!

Quirks

With all its quirks
Life still works!

Happenings

It'll happen if it should
If it doesn't...
Maybe you should prepare better!

Confusion

When
Confusion
Reigns...
Pour on
Calmness

Importance

You define your own importance!

Success and Failure

Dwelling on your successes
May be prideful, however...

Dwelling on your failures
May be motivation for success!

Your Problems

Even the darkest clouds
Are beautiful from above...

Visualize the reward on the
Other side of your problems

And then figure out
A way to solve them.

Any Problems

If it wasn't for problems

There'd be no solutions!

Goal Achievement

To get from here to there
Takes more than hot air
It takes persistence
And even insistence

I insist
You persist!

Over There

It's gotta be better over there...
Believe me, I'd go on a dare

But, when I look a bit more near
I see them people a' lookin' here

<u>Your</u> Journey

To prepare
For each day's journey
Make sure your brain is well
Connected to your nervous system

Wisdom:

Sometimes
It takes a bit of wit
To make wisdom stick!

Surprises

Surprises
Are good for you.
They quicken the heart
And sharpen your reflexes.
Sometimes they exercise the brain!

More importantly, it is prudent to be
Prepared for them, as the following
Inspiration for this entry will attest to.

A 1:00 AM prowler tried one of our windows last night. Good thing he was scared off when our live in friend turned on the bedroom light. A snub nosed 38 would have been an unpleasant surprise for him, I suspect. We called the police. They responded and were pleased that we had deterrent power. They inspected the area and then patrolled the neighborhood. We were grateful for their presence!

As the 18th century old Quaker told an intruder in the middle of the night: Friend... I would not harm thee for the world, but **thee is standing where I am about to shoot!!**

(The Quaker response is taken from a story in the book: *"Laughter in Quaker Grey"*)

Jim Haworth

Lessons

There's a lesson to be learned,

Every time you get Burned!

Disappointment

Disappointment comes in many ways.
Sometimes it even lasts for days

It usually hurts more to disappoint someone else
A lot more than it does to disappoint yourself.

Sometimes a slip-up, not meant,
Results in a world of discontent.

Having a quick discourse
Can cure it at the source.

The value of this lesson
Can be a lifelong Blessin'!

You've got a brain...

The cigarette doesn't...
Who should be in control???!

Blessings

Each day
Is a Blessing.
Sometimes it's
Hard to understand...
But it's worth the effort.

When Work is no Longer Fun

When work
Is no longer fun,
It is definitely work.
So, try to keep it fun!!!

Challenged?

**With pluck, I can try...
With perseverance, I can do!**

When you can't go any farther

When you can't go any farther...
Exit the safety module
And fly away!

Picture of an empty Cicada exoskeleton:

Youth

A time of irreverence, brashness and hormones.
Mix it with alcohol and they'll jump your bones

For sensibility is low in a daze
Of the alcohol induced haze

And if you add pot,
It decreases a lot

I may not be very sage,
But I advise the underage:

Keep it straight,
Don't tempt fate!

You are
The sum of
All your experience
Take advantage of that!

Life Happens

Life happens every day
Be sure to catch it
Before it zips away

Life is Too

Life is
Too short
Not to learn

But Most of All...

But,
Most
Of all...

Don't forget
To read the comics!

Chapter Seven
Dichotomy & Other Persasions

Dichotomy

The dichotomy
Of life is pervasive!

The Dichotamous Care Giver

My wife recently had a bad reaction to a new medication prescribed by her physician. It left her very fatigued almost to the point of being non-responsive. Additionally there were affects on her memory and her ability to hold objects. Dinner was an experience which we will laugh about later. Much later!

One afternoon I had to get her ready for a family visit. The struggle was successful, and we had a good, though subdued visit. Afterwards I was surprised to hear my wife say "It took two of you to get me ready for our visit. I thought about this for a moment and said "Both of them were me... the gentle one to coax you into getting going, and the hard-ass one to prod you along firmly!"

Life may require you to be more than one person. And, sometimes those people must serve at the same time.

The Path

The path of least resistance
Is often a much less scenic one.

Trust

Life, Trust and Love are complimentary.

In a world where trust and love is in the heart of
all men, there'd be no reason for prisons and wars.

The Dichotomy of Chocolate

Chocolate tastes GREAT...
Early or late

There's no such thing
As chocolittle.

There's only chocoLOT!

It's an irrefutable fact:

Chocolate is one of the staples of life.
One's place on the chocolate graph of life
is deter-mined by the available supply
and the strength of one's dedication
to resisting over-indulgence.

Nice Thoughts or Not

If
You
Can't
Think of
Anything nice
To say, then just
Think of nice things till
Something comes to mind and
By then things might cool down a bit.

Life is a Series

Life is a series of Mondays...
Or is it maybe of Saturdays...

It depends upon your point of view
Of what makes you happy or blue

A Good Idea

A good idea
Is only good if
It is acted upon!

A Famous Writer Once Said...

The best
Laid plans
Of mice and
Men oft go awry

  But Simon Sez:
  You've got a far better chance as a man!

A Picture May Be...

A picture may be worth a thousand words
But the imagination behind it is priceless
And the discussion about it may be endless!

Learn!

Learn from the past
And get it right at last!

Short Fuse (1)

If you didn't have such a short fuse
You might not be singing the blues!

A Smile May Be

A smile may be
Fleeting on the lips,
But it is forever in the heart.

No man is an island

While no man is an island,
He harbors an island within.

Control Implies

Control implies limits
Which implies stasis
Which implies stagnation
Which implies stiffled imagination
Which implies lack of forward progress
Which implies a need for maliable control
And interactive feedback and communication

Success & Opportunity

Measure
Success by
How well you
Handle failures

Life gaurantees

you will have that

Opportunity!

Chapter Eight
Acronyms to live by
(Taken from Simon Sez: You're the Expert on You)

ATTITUDE

Always

Try

To

Infuse

The

Unadulterated best

Darn

Effort into it all!

Respect

Rarely
Expressed
Sufficiently, but everyone
Prefers it and
Expects it
Consistently
Today

COURAGE

Calm action when
Others don't react to the
Urgent need to
Respond immediately to
Arrest the progress of a
Growing danger or
Even potentially fatal event.

*Instinctive reactions sometimes are considered
Courageous, but not by the person who acted.*

EXERCISE

Everyone, except maybe
Xerxes, needs to exercise
Every day to
Render the fat and
Create improved circulation. This
Includes
Slim and not so slim folks slowly
Evolving to better health

Excellence

Exclusive of those already in
Xanadu, we should all
Cultivate the habit of achieving
Excellence in our daily
Lives, striving to
Learn more
Effective ways to
Navigate the
Course of
Each day's endeavors

INTEGRITY

In an ideal world
No one would ever
Tell anyone
Even the most juicy
Gossip or untruth
Related to another to
Ingratiate themselves
To another, or to
You

Let's try to make it so!

NOTORIETY

No one wants
Others
To see them as...
Or to
Really be... that
Incorrigible, and yet
Everyone secretly thinks
That it would be fun for
You to be a little notorious

PASSION*

Passion
Accentuates all
Serious
Success stories
Independent
Of category or person,
Now, in the past or the future

*Written for Lori Pierce, who says it's her favorite word.

POSITIVE

Positive people
Often
Show a positive attitude
Intentionally so
That it will
Influence
Virtually
Everyone, including themselves

It usually works (kind 'a like smiles)

PERSONALITY

People
Everywhere
Rarely
Seek out
Others with
Negative personality
Attributes, so
Light up your
Inner person such
That especially today
You glow outwardly

(You never know whose life you may change forever!)

UPBEAT

Unless you actually
Prefer to
Be morose, you should
Exert every effort to
Achieve happiness
Throughout your life

Risk

Really

Important

Stuff to

Know

Whether it impacts your
health or financial wellbeing!

CHANCE

Chances are you'll never

Have a second chance for

A first impression so be

Nice on the first encounter

Concentrating on the

Essentials that matter.

Chance is like serendipity. It strikes when
you least expect it. So be prepared to go
with the flow with a positive attitude.

SUPPORT

Sincere and
Unrestricted
Personal consideration of
Putting (or keeping)
Others needs in mind
Rarely is a burden
That weighs heavily

MEMORY

Memory is so precious...
Everyone needs it
More as they get
Older, but that's when
Remembering is harder
Year after year... HELP!!!

(Just like a hard drive that gets slow when it's full)

RESPONSIBILITY

Resolve
Every
Serious
Problem
Or
Negotiate
Some
Improvement
Before
It becomes a
Lost
Investment of
Time and
Your patience

THANKSGIVING

Thank
Heaven
Above and
Never
Keep
Something
Gnawing
Inside, for
Verily
I say, forgiving is a
Necessary part of
Giving thanks

Think about it and then do it.

Chapter Nine
Impatience

Impatience May...

Impatience
Sometimes takes
Looooooooooooooooooonger!

Impatience May Not...

Impatience may not be a four-letter word,
But it often begets and elicits them in quantity

Impatience used right...

Impatience used right may
Teach the art of being patient.

Patience Allows...

Patience allows you
To savor the flavor

A short cut here, a short cut there...

A short cut here,
A short cut there...
May result in less input
And less enjoyment out of life
(Doesn't give you much time to smell the roses along the way)

A Short Fuse (2)
Doesn't give you much time to think!

Sometimes...

Sometimes
You just gotta
Stare off into space
With your eyes closed,
To get through it... y'know?

Chapter Ten
Patience

Patience
Allows you to
Push past obstacles

What else can I say?

Chapter Eleven
Time

Time... Never say

Never say you don't have enough time...
There's plenty of time... it goes on forever

The problem is, there's not enough of you...So, use it
while you can and make the most of it!

Time is like

Time is like change
It never stops!

Life's Short

Life's short
The longer you live
The shorter it gets

Time off

If you're tired and at a loss
You better get some time off

For in this time and age,
You need more than a wage

No matter what...Come what may,
Make sure you get some time to play

Time is on Loan

Time may be
On loan from God
It is not ours to keep-
But we still need to sleep

Time is Never Lost

Time is
Never lost
It's just misused

Time is to be

Time is to be
Used not abused

Time Travels

Time
Travels
The same
We just use
It with different
Degrees of efficiency

Time is the constant:
Our ability to
Deal with it
Is the variable!

Time is relative

Time is relative
And some relatives
Require too much time!

Time Challenges

Challenges come on Monday
So you have time
To get over
Them
Before
Saturday

If Time Stood Still

If Time Stood Still
So would we!

Chapter Twelve
Getting Old

Old Age is When...

Old Age is
When you get those
Sprinkles of wrinkles!

Old Folks Are Like...

Old
Folks
Are like
Astronauts
They have to
Hold on to stuff
To get around space

Getting Old Reminds us That...

Any
Endeavor
Worthy of doing
Is worthy of repeating
Unfortunately, we repeat a lot

Keeping Busy

**Keeping Busy
Is Staying Alive!**

**Being Bold
Should Never
Ever Get Old!**

Persistence

**Getting old is
A form of persistence!
And don't you ever forget it!**

The Older You Get

**The
Older
You get
The less you
Tolerate solicitation:
Hang up with no hesitation!**

If old is...

If old is a
Matter of your
Prejudicial attitude
It's time to get a new one!

Old, the Perspective

From here to old
Is a matter of perspective
For me, it's a very long way off

Old age... the short version:

Impatience
May just shorten
Your trip to old age!

If You're New to Old Age...

I hope the trip
Took a long time
And was a lot of fun!

Old: The Age of Solicitation

If being
Solicitated, then
Return the favor by
Pushing your own agenda
On your intrusive, insistant caller!

Old Can Be...

Old can be the new
Age of discovery and awe!

If You've Spent

If you've spent a lot of time
Getting to Old Age
Are you sure
You are
There
Yet?

If Old Age is

If Old Age is getting old for you...
Don't worry... You'll get over it!

And these are my final words on the subject:

I
AM
Not Old
I am Now!

As
Long
As you
Can live
You can love!

Inspired by a conversation with Nurse Lee Ann Throm, retired from St. Vincent. Hospital, Indianapolis Indiana

The Birthday Concept

Simon Sez:

Birthdays may be a transient concept...

But they last as long as it takes...
So, enjoy and keep on goin'

"Cause...

He who laughs last
Lives longest!

And, has a

Happy
Birth
Day

The Older we get, Part Two

The older
We get, the more
We have... to think about.

Think <u>that</u> for a minute or an hour!

You ever see a picture of a great
Thinker that wasn't old?
Well, there you are!
It's never too late
To get started or
To continue!

Chapter Thirteen
Where do we go from here

Step One

Find out where you want to go,
Or you can't get there... PERIOD!

Step Two

Decide if this is to be
A life goal for eternity
Or a dalliance along the way

Step Three

Study the options
And make a plan

Step Four

Make sure you've
Got what you need
To start the plan

Step Five

Review the plan for practicality...
Ask your self this important question:
What the heck am I doing (and why!)

Step Six

Make your first move
Get your butt in gear!

Step Seven

Find someone to
Talk you out of it.

Step Eight

If they talk you out of it
Plan to go somewhere else

Step Nine

If not maybe they'll
Help you to get there!

Along The Way

Life is not only about evaluating the bumps along the way,
But it's also about enjoying them to the fullest that you can.

Inspired by Steve Zepfan.

Life is a Series of Habits

Life is a series of habits that are
Interspersed with spontaneity

Fulfillment comes from
Immersing yourself in both

Lessons

Lessons
From the past
Shape the future...

Unfortunately...

Ignoring those lessons
From the past <u>also</u> shapes it!

Aren't you Glad?

The mind is like each card in the deck.
It's a good thing there's a cover on it!

So, We Gotta...

Too soon the good days get old... so,
We just gotta keep making new ones.

Inspired by Kay Dull, also retired from
St. Vincent Hospital, Indianapolis Indiana

Empathy

Empathy
Is essential to
A successful future

Connections

Making
Connections
Is the easy part.
Sustaining them is
The important part!

Fertilize it

I have a tree fertilizer.
He walks with me every day.
He helps give springtime a boost!

The Final Frontier

The final frontier
can be unlocked by
the power of the mind.
The mind, attitude and will,
Can drive you on roads
You never perceived.

Chapter Fourteen
I Can't Get It Out of My Head!

The Mind

The
Mind
Is a trap:
It keeps stuff
You'd rather lose.

On
The
Other
Hand,
It can be
A sieve that
Let's out some
Stuff you wanted.

Maybe you just need to
Practice better mind control

The Schedule!

How wonderful is the schedule!
An awesome indispensable tool

It tells you when and where to be
Even in the midst of ocean or sea

And yet coordination of these fabulous jewels
May seem like the passionate work of fools!

For the change of one single element in space
Can set a cascade of myriad changes in place!

The schedule, the schedule, that cantankerous tool...
Still beats 100 monkeys and typewriters by the pool!

Depressed?

Clean
Your sink
Till it sparkles.
You'll feel better!
No? So, do another!
Didn't work? Keep at it.
Soon the house will be clean,
And you can take a nap and when
You wake up refreshed, you'll feel better.
Me? Yeah, I stopped at the sink and felt better!

Chapter Fifteen
Warnings

Control

An overbearing
Control tends to stifle
The entrepreneurial spirit,
Except in the area of rebellion...
Where it is an accelerator of action!

Cocaine!

Coke! Coke! It's no joke!
It'll leave you broke!

In more ways than one!!

Do You Smoke?

Suicide by cigarette
A trip you'll regret

Bit by bit, piece by piece
Your body gets released

A blood vessel here 'n there
You're falling apart everywhere!

Soon you start wheezin'...
Trouble with yer breathin'

The blood has trouble getting' to yer legs
"Help me get rid of this pain!" ya begs.

Then at last, or maybe first:
"Oh God! My chest hurts!"

Did you really need that heart?
Smoking just wasn't so smart!

And when at last they lower you down
You enter a smoke free underground

You might say it was just
The early return to dust!

I can talk about this because I used to smoke.
I was smart... I quit in 1967.

The Physics of Fat

Einstein wrote about relativity
And the conservation of energy

A body at rest
Tends to stay at rest

A body on the go
Tends to remain so

From China to ancient Persia
This is described as inertia

A body at rest stores energy as fat
So, in need, it'll know where it's at

A body on the go removes that fat
'Cause it remembers where it's at.

So, here's a timely word to the wise:
Ya better not leave it on your thighs!

Your Marvelous Machine

It's one that each and all have seen
This absolutely fabulous machine!

Your body is practically perfection
It works under most any condition

Its working range is wide and varied,
So you can function slowly or harried

But even so, its limits can be exceeded
And then medical attention is needed.

Be very careful in what you do
So this doesn't happen to you!

Impending and Unending?

Got that feeling of impending reality?
Like there will soon be an unpleasant situation?

Take another serious look at your to do list for today.
Did you update it with all those past undone to do things?

When you've completed that updated list, check those feelings again.

I've got a feeling that feeling of doom will be gone and you feel better already!

The Past

Forget
The past, it's
Done and gone.
Keep, however,
Its lessons
<u>Forever!</u>

Using Connections

Using
Connections
Requires education,
Understanding, confidence
Faith and willingness, both in yourself,
The situation and the other parties as well.

True Friends

True
Friends
Weather the
Rigors of Time
Stress and Distance:
True friendship surpasses!

Update Your Past

We need to update
The door to the past,

> To look for the beauty,
> Wisdom and strength

That we may find in our past,
The memories, associations and

> Learning experiences so necessary
> To aid us in facing future changes.

The Past Has a Way of...

The past has a way
Of catching up with you

So, to be prepared for it...
Work faster on your future!

Chapter Seventeen
At Last!

I Died the Other Day (more humor)

I died the other day...
I don't know why, it just happened that way

One minute I was talking on the phone,
The next minute I was lying prone!

As I was lying on the floor,
Totally unable to implore,

I saw my wife come in from the car...
Too bad I never taught her CPR!

As she entered the room,
She began to swoon!

Then she hung up on the caller,
Dialed 911 and began to holler!

I watched the rescue from the ceiling
As down the street they were pealing

They got out the paddles, ripped open my shirt
And when they zapped me, it didn't even hurt!

Punching and jabbing, they gave me drugs
While a neighbor gave my wife big hugs.

I knew my fate:
They were too late!

Well, we had made our plans ahead of time
There'd be no caskets, neither her's nor mine.

Our selection for heavenly initiation
Would most definitely be cremation.

When the flames got hotter, I could tell,
My remains were looking quite skeletal!

As the smoke cleared from the air
Only the ashes were still left there.

But the story doesn't end quite there...
For I'm going to be a diamond solitaire!

My wife gave a great big old bash
To celebrate my conversion from ash.

Family and neighbors with many a friend
Partied to celebrate my life and its final end.

As I watched, (and I love this part the best),
She showed me off, sparkling on her chest!

Did you know that you really can have your ashes
Heated and compressed to become a diamond?

Yes... you can!

Seasonal Thoughts

The Three Great Things About Summer

1. Basking in the sun
2. Hiking in the woods
3. Having a cook out for no reason

The Three Great Things About Fall

1. The smell of burning leaves
2. Cool evenings to sit on the porch
3. Hot dogs, S'mores and cold cider

The Three Great Things About Snow:

1. Watching it fall
2. Playing in it
3. Watching it leave!!

The Three Great Things About Spring

1. Stomping in rain puddles
2. The smell of fresh mowed grass
3. Flowers busting out all over!

*I couldn't leave you with thoughts of snow at the end
Of this book! You always gotta look forward to rebirth:
Spring flowers in bloom to freshen your mind's rooms!*

Time for Introspection...

Questions for Your Inner You:

Are you really at peace
In this body you lease?

Does your outer face
Reflect your inner space?
Do you stop playing hero or clown?
And take time to center down?

Do you spend your time wisely, then,
To hear that still small voice within?

When you've thought this thought,
Then do you do what you ought?

Will your conscience be your goad,
For when the rubber hits the road?

If you'll do
This for you,

You'll find
Peace of mind.

Chapter Eighteen
Consider God

The God Addiction

If ya gotta be addicted,
Be addicted to God!

If you're into addictions,
Choose to be addicted to God.

If you like addictions,
Choose the God addiction.

If you're into that addiction thing
Why not put God into your ring?

The God addiction:

Once you're hooked,
Ya can't be cooked!!

God Put You There

God
put you
where you are
For a reason

Learn
Teach and help
Until He is satisfied

If God Were Part of Your Body...

If God were part of your body...
What part would he be?

He'd be your blood, permeating
Every single cell in your body.

He supplies the good stuff
And removes the bad stuff.

Nature

Though we love parts of her,
we are not in a loving relationship...

She, given a chance... would dominate, subdue and eliminate us.

So, it is not incumbent upon us to give her that chance, but to...

Practice a symbiotic relationship to the point of perfection...

In such a manner, as to please our mutual Maker with praise.

Life's End

God designed our bodies
With built in wear dates

So, we'll be ready and willing
To leave them...*When He calls us*

Follow the Light
To that Ultimate Door

**Not
Everyone
Will percieve it
In the same way...**

The Ultimate Door

Stretch for it

It may be a stretch,
But striving for the light
Is always right.

Reaching for the light

My Other Books*

2006
**Wit and Wisdom from the Wild and Wacky
World of Simon Stargazer III**

2009
Simon Sez: You're the Expert on You!

2011
**Simon Sez: A Glass Half Full or
Half Empty, still is Enough
For a Good Drink!**

2012
**Simon Sez: The Future or Bust!
Getting Past the End of the Mayan Calendar
(As Simon Stargazer III sees it),**

In the not too distant future:
Simon's Anthology of Sci/Fi and Fantasy

The book you just read contains occasional
excerpts from these other four books...I'll bet
a few of you may remember reading them. Do
you remember which book they came from?

About the Author

Mr. Haworth was born in Arbuckle California in 1941. He lived in many states in what you might call an eclectic life. With eight brothers from his parent's various marriages, he quickly learned how to deal with life's challenges.

After graduating from a Quaker College with a Biology degree and a minor in Religion, Jim went to work in the medical field. After a short stent working in a mental hospital, he began work at St. Vincent Hospital in Indianapolis, becoming deeply involved with the growing field of Ultrasound in its various iterations, including Cardiology, Neurology, Obstetrics, Gynecology and Vascular Technology.

A fifty-year career in the medical field, coupled with life in diverse parts of the country, makes him uniquely qualified to present an array of short, but to the point, thoughts on living life and enjoying it while pursuing success.

In 1984, he discovered his talent for writing when he bought his first Macintosh computer. He began seriously writing his short thoughts and Sci-Fi stories around 1999, delving into poetry a few years later. In this way he began to express his positive thoughts on life. For several years, he gathered them together presenting them to his children at Christmas time.

In 2006, he organized his writings and published his first inspirational book. He's been at it ever since. This is book number five. Book six is already under way.

Positive thoughts Once a Week

To get positive thoughts once week by e-mail,
send me an e-mail to:

Simonstargazer@gmail.com
with **Positive Thoughts** as the subject.
There is no charge

And consider this about perception...

Perception
Is rarely reality, but it
Sometimes leads to a real future.

Simon Stargazer III

Thanks for buying my book(s)
And taking the time to read them.
I hope it was time well spent.
Feel free to share
With others.

Jim Haworth

Printed in the United States
By Bookmasters